# Nashua Public Library

## Enjoy this book!
Please remember to return it on time
so that others may enjoy it too.

Manage your library account and
discover all we offer by visiting us
online at www.nashualibrary.org

**Love your library? Tell a friend!**

J

My First Pet

# Rats

by Vanessa Black

Bullfrog Books

# Ideas for Parents and Teachers

Bullfrog Books let children practice reading informational text at the earliest reading levels. Repetition, familiar words, and photo labels support early readers.

## Before Reading
- Discuss the cover photo. What does it tell them?
- Look at the picture glossary together. Read and discuss the words.

## Read the Book
- "Walk" through the book and look at the photos. Let the child ask questions. Point out the photo labels.
- Read the book to the child, or have him or her read independently.

## After Reading
- Prompt the child to think more. Ask: What do you need to take care of a rat? Would you like one as a pet?

Bullfrog Books are published by Jump!
5357 Penn Avenue South
Minneapolis, MN 55419
www.jumplibrary.com

Library of Congress Cataloging-in-Publication Data

Names: Black, Vanessa, author.
Title: Rats / by Vanessa Black.
Description: Minneapolis, MN: Jump!, Inc., [2017]
Series: My first pet | Audience: Age 5–8.
Audience: K to grade 3.
Includes bibliographical references and index.
Identifiers: LCCN 2016029346 (print)
LCCN 2016029928 (ebook)
ISBN 9781620315545 (hardcover: alk. paper)
ISBN 9781624965029 (ebook)
Subjects: LCSH: Rats as pets—Juvenile literature.
Rats—Juvenile literature.
Classification: LCC SF459.R3 B53 2017 (print)
LCC SF459.R3 (ebook) | DDC 636.935/2—dc23
LC record available at https://lccn.loc.gov/2016029346

Editor: Kirsten Chang
Book Designer: Michelle Sonnek
Photo Researcher: Michelle Sonnek

Photo Credits: All photos by Shutterstock except:
Adobe Stock, 12–13; Alamy 6–7, 13, 20–21, 23tr;
Dreamstime, 8–9; Getty, 14–15; Kimball Stock,
10, 23tl; Superstock, 24.

Printed in the United States of America at
Corporate Graphics in North Mankato, Minnesota.

# Table of Contents

# A New Pet

Sven wants a pet.

He gets a rat.

A rat is a social animal.
Mary has two rats.
She plays with them.
They play together.

# A rat likes to climb.
# Penny has a tall cage.

cage

A rat is curious.

Darcy takes Hugs out.

She lets him explore.

She gives him toys.

A rat can do tricks.
Ratty runs
across a rope.
Spike climbs
up a ladder.
He climbs down.

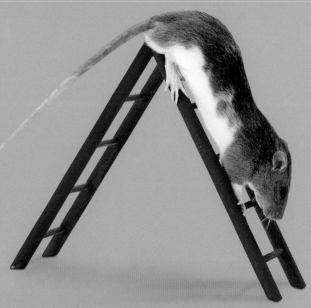

A rat runs.

Ned uses a wheel.

A rat chews.

Ron gives Rio sticks to chew.

If he doesn't chew, his teeth grow too long.

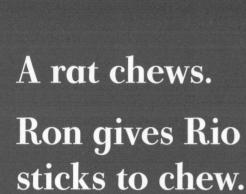

chew sticks

teeth

Sometimes, a rat gets sick.

Kira takes Ren to the vet.

He gets medicine.

medicine

**All better!**

# Rats are cool pets!

# What Does a Rat Need?

**cage**
Rats need a large space to live in.

**bedding**
Rats need bedding; provide paper pellet or shredded cardboard bedding, never cedar or pine.

**toys**
Rats need to play with toys so they don't get bored.

**food and water**
Rats get nutrients from special pellets and fresh veggies. They need fresh water every day.

# Picture Glossary

**curious**
Eager to
learn about
something.

**social**
To enjoy
being around
other people
and animals.

**medicine**
Something
(often a liquid
or pills) used
to relieve pain
or cure sickness.

**vet**
An animal
doctor.

# Index

# To Learn More

Learning more is as easy as 1, 2, 3.

1) Go to www.factsurfer.com

2) Enter "petrats" into the search box.

3) Click the "Surf" button to see a list of websites.

With factsurfer.com, finding more information is just a click away.